Original title:

A Slice of the Tropics

Copyright © 2025 Creative Arts Management OÜ

All rights reserved.

Author: Gideon Shaw

ISBN HARDBACK: 978-1-80581-526-6

ISBN PAPERBACK: 978-1-80581-053-7

ISBN EBOOK: 978-1-80581-526-6

Radiant Estuary

In the mangroves, crabs do dance,
They've got moves that leave you in a trance.
Pelicans dive, missing their perfect catch,
Leaving fish giggling, giving a cheerful scratch.

Sunsets splash colors on the surface bright,
Seagulls squawking, taking their flight.
Fishermen joke about their glorious fails,
While in the distance, a dolphin wails.

Painted Skies

Clouds like cotton candy floating so high,
Making us ponder if we can touch the sky.
Parrots squawk jokes that tickle our ears,
As we sip coconut water and hide our fears.

The sun winks down with a cheeky grin,
While flip-flops chase us as we dash in.
Here rent is cheap, but laughter's a treasure,
Finding joy in moments—our ultimate measure.

Laughter of the Waves

Waves roll in with a giggle and roar,
Tumbling shells like they're coming for more.
Sandcastles crumble, but never lose cheer,
As seaweed tickles while the tide draws near.

Surfers wipe out—it's all part of the game,
With splashes and chuckles, who's really to blame?
Sunbathers grin in their slippery lotion,
As a funny crab scuttles in awkward motion.

Secrets in the Underbrush

In the thick greens, secrets begin to stir,
A rabbit in shades of bright, dancing fur.
Whispers of laughter creep through the air,
As tiny frogs leap without a care.

Snakes with sunglasses lounging in style,
Plotting their next move, but not for a while.
Fireflies wink like they're up to some tricks,
While lizards join in for a comedy mix.

Sunset Over Turquoise Waves

The sun dips low, a ball of fire,
Seagulls squawk, their screeches dire.
A crab in shorts, he scuttles past,
Looking for lunch, he's such a blast!

Flip-flops fly as kids do race,
Into the waves, a splashy chase.
A sandy dog rolls on the shore,
Wagging his tail, he begs for more!

Whispering Palms Beneath Starlit Skies

The palms lean in, they share a tale,
Of a dancing girl who drank too pale.
She tripped on roots, fell with a plop,
While snickers rose from those who bop.

The stars above just winked and swayed,
As crickets chirped, the night parade.
With coconuts as makeshift hats,
They laughed and danced like silly cats!

Mango Dreams Under a Coconut Canopy

A mango slipped, oh what a sight,
It knocked a guy, now there's a fight!
He blames the fruit, the fruit's to blame,
For turning joggers into fame!

Under the shade, the coconuts grin,
While ants hold a feast, they all dig in.
A parrot squawks, "Watch out below!"
But everyone knows he's in the show!

The Rhythm of Island Rain

Raindrops fall like peppy drums,
The tourist slips, and down he hums.
Umbrellas flip like flopping fish,
While locals laugh, fulfill their wish.

The puddles form a dance floor wet,
With splashes loud, they won't forget.
A frog leaps high, he steals the show,
In rhythm with the rain, oh go, frog, go!

Moonlit Canopy

Under starlit laughter, trees play peek-a-boo,
Chasing shadows, the night's a comedy crew.
The coconuts giggle, swaying side to side,
As the moon rolls its eyes, on this wild joyride.

Crickets sing jokes in a rhythm so sweet,
While the owls roll their eyes and admit defeat.
Palm fronds wave hello, with a cheeky swirl,
As if nature's saying, 'Let's give it a whirl!'

Gentle Currents

Waves tickle sand like a playful old friend,
With a splash and a laugh, their antics won't end.
Seagulls squawk puns as they dive with such flair,
Each fish jumps up, like, 'Did you see that air?'

The sun dons a cap, ready for a swim,
As shells whisper tales of seafoam and whim.
In this bubbly playground, the tides take their turn,
And everyone's dancing, it's a splashy concern!

Banter of the Breeze

Breezes tug at hats, with a mischievous grin,
Whispering secrets of the island's din.
Feathery palms gossip in a rustling tone,
While flowers blush red, feeling a bit known.

Kites soar high, teasing clouds in the sky,
As the sun giggles softly, giving it a try.
Wind plays tag with a carefree delight,
In this tropical mix, everything feels right!

Timeless Shores

Footprints in sand lead a story to tell,
Of a crab's sassy dance and a seashell's swell.
The tide rolls in, with a wink and a nod,
Gathering whispers from the beachside squad.

Sunhats tip over, laughing at the sun,
While flip-flops gossip, the fun's just begun.
With each wave that crashes, joy spills on the sand,
As the ocean joins in, to form a happy band!

Honey Dripping from Papaya Trees

In a field where the fruit all swaggers,
Lemonade rains like fortune from wagons,
Bees wear tiny hats and race like ninjas,
While ants throw parties, dancing in their linens.

Papayas waddle, flaunting their smooth skins,
With secrets hidden where the sweet life begins,
Chickens cluck gossip about falling pears,
While pigs in sunglasses bask in their cares.

Friendly boa constrictors serve as slides,
Where kids take turns, not fearing who rides,
Laughter blooms like flowers in bright attire,
As monkeys juggle fruit above a campfire.

So grab a plate, let's feast with a grin,
On this orchard stage, let the fun begin,
With honey dripping, laughter free as air,
We'll toast to life as sweet as a clementine fair.

The Call of the Singing Parrots

Up in the trees where the colors collide,
Parrots plot mischief, full of pride,
They squawk about love like it's breaking news,
While flirting with toucans in vibrant hues.

Oh, what a choir, a loud, feathery mess,
Each note a riddle, a puzzling guess,
They challenge each other to sing their best,
But end up tangled in their feathery vest.

One parrot declares, 'I can croon a tune!'
While the others mimic under the moon,
They laugh and they squawk, a raucous parade,
With melodies strange, a comical charade.

The jungle's alive with their colorful chatter,
While the shy sloths wonder, "What's all the clatter?"
Each day is a concert, a splash of delight,
As the parrots take center stage, ready to ignite.

Beneath the Banyan's Embrace

Under a banyan, secrets unfurl,
Where squirrels sip tea and the turtles swirl,
Lemurs plot capers, all sneaky and spry,
While the groundhogs giggle and pass by.

The roots twist like snakes in a playful dance,
While frogs wear top hats, not leaving to chance,
They leap for the sky with each whimsical twirl,
Creating a party that makes hearts whirl.

Old owls debate on who's the wisest there,
And fireflies flash like they just don't care,
The shadows grow long in the fading light,
As the jungle erupts into laughter and flight.

So join in the fun when dusk falls near,
With tales spun of mischief, seasoned with cheer,
Beneath the banyan, where dreams take flight,
Life's little wonders will make the night bright.

Starlight Reflections on Still Waters

On a pond where starlight glimmers and plays,
Frogs put on tuxedos for evening displays,
They sing their best croaks to the moon's glowing face,
While dragonflies compete in a dance-off race.

Fish wear bow ties as they splash about,
Creating ripples that dance and shout,
"Join us, dear friends, in this water ballet!"
As crickets applaud, the stars join the fray.

Reflections hold secrets, like whispers in dreams,
Bubbles of laughter burst at the seams,
Who knew such wonders could float on the breeze,
As the night wraps in laughter like curtains with ease?

So come take a dive, splash the night away,
In this watery realm where mischief holds sway,
With starlit reflections, a whimsical sight,
We'll toast to the chaos that makes life so bright.

Whispering Waves

The ocean giggles as it splashes,
A crab in a tux makes dapper dashes.
Seagulls squawk jokes, they can't seem to quit,
While beach balls bounce like a comedic skit.

Bikini-clad folks tumble and fall,
Suntan lotion launched—what a mishap call!
Flip-flops fly in a whimsical dance,
As laughter erupts, giving chaos a chance.

Snorkelers gaze, imagining fish,
One catches a boot—what a curious dish.
The sun sets low with a wink and a grin,
As the day ends with a giggle-filled spin.

Nature's Palette

Bright hues paint the jungle, oh so loud,
A parrot shouts jokes, drawing a crowd.
Monkeys wear hats made of leaves just in style,
Bouncing around, they bring laughter for miles.

Coconuts drop, a rhythmic thud,
One lands on a pig—it's an instant dud.
The flowers compete in a vibrant array,
Blooming with laughter like it's a cabaret.

Vines wrap around creatures in playful binds,
As frogs do a jig that truly unwinds.
Amidst quirky critters, all fun and all free,
Nature's a comedian, just wait and see!

Sanctuary of the Skies

Clouds drift on by, looking like sheep,
While a bird on a wire starts to sing and leap.
The sun wears shades, oh what a cool cat,
As kites dance high, like they're doing the chat.

Breezes do waltzes, playful and light,
Tickling the cheeks, oh what a delight.
A toucan tells tales with a giggle in tow,
As rainbows of laughter in the skies flow.

Stars tease the moon, telling secrets at night,
While owls drop puns that take flight with delight.
In the sanctuary where the sky holds its glee,
Every moment's a joke, how playful are we!

Harmony of Hibiscus

Hibiscus blooms in a riot of cheer,
A flower so funny, it cracks up the deer.
Bumblebees buzzing with humor so sweet,
Join in the fun as they dance on their feet.

A gardener sings to his plants with a grin,
They giggle back gently, coaxing each win.
Lizards in sunglasses lounge in the sun,
Sunbathing iguanas invite everyone.

As laughter erupts from the petals in bloom,
The fragrance of joy creates a sweet room.
In this garden of quips, nature's light-hearted,
Every blossom knows when the day just started.

Mango Haze

In the sun, I munch my fruit,
Juicy splatters, what a hoot!
A mango dribble on my chin,
Looks like I'm losing—again!

Sticky fingers, laughter out,
My friends all tease and laugh about.
We're painting faces with the juice,
Mango mayhem, what a ruse!

Mosquitoes dance, they buzz and prance,
Who invited them to this tropical dance?
But with each bite, I spot a joke,
Laughter blooms, like a funny cloak.

So here we sit, a silly crew,
In this golden, fruity zoo.
With rain and shine, we slice the fun,
Mango dreams under the sun!

Dancing Palms

Palm trees shimmy in the breeze,
Looking like they're dancing, if you please!
One leans right, the other sways left,
Two groovy pals, they're quite deft!

Beach balls bounce, they roll downhill,
Chasing them is quite a thrill.
Sunburn marks where I have been,
I look like I wrestled with a tin!

Sandcastles stretch up to the sky,
Then get knocked down—oh me, oh my!
The palm trunks chuckle as we flee,
Building dreams in sandy glee.

Under sun hats, smiles wide,
With wild fun, we cannot hide.
A tropical day wrapped in cheer,
Let's dance with palm trees, bring a beer!

Coral Mirage

Beneath the waves, a bright surprise,
Coral reefs with silly ties.
Fish in tuxedos swim and play,
A joyful ballet in the bay!

Shrimp with shades are looking cool,
They host the party in this pool.
"Let's dance!" they say, with graceful swirls,
"Forget your worries, just do twirls!"

Jellyfish wear hats with flair,
Wobbling along without a care.
I slip and slide in flippers wide,
As laughter echoes, our goofy guide.

At the shore, we trade our tales,
Of underwater, fruit-filled gales.
Coral won't mind if we're a bit mad,
In this mirage, we'll all be glad!

Breeze of Paradise

A gentle wind brings scents so sweet,
Coconut and laughter meet.
My hat flies off, it takes a chance,
The breeze has started quite a dance!

Sipping drinks with little umbrellas,
We spot some clumsy, wobbly fella's.
Stumbling by with a grin so wide,
He trips on sand, but can't decide!

Seagulls squawk and steal my fries,
Stepping back, catching my sighs.
Yet every bite becomes a feast,
With beachside antics, we're all released.

Under sunbeams, we sing out loud,
Fun in the chaos—not allowed!
The breeze of joy brings us delight,
In this paradise, we take flight!

The Magic of Sun-Baked Skin

When the sun kisses my back, oh my,
I turn into a lobster, oh my, oh my!
I'll wear SPF like a badge of pride,
But still end up a shade of fried.

My friends all laugh as I hobble 'round,
Like a crab with complications, I'm bound.
They slather lotion on my sunburned space,
Saying, "You should've stayed home, just in case!"

With coconut drinks in our hands, we cheer,
But my peeling skin? It's the real souvenir.
Dance like nobody's watching the scene,
Dodging the beach ball, in my sunscreen sheen.

Island Echoes in a Twilight Breeze

The waves whisper gossip, secrets they keep,
While seagulls caw tales that interrupt sleep.
I shout back in laughter, what a delight!
The stars roll their eyes, it's quite the sight.

Crabs play connect-the-dots on the sand,
As I lose my flip-flop, a true reprimand.
The breeze brings me laughter, a funny embrace,
I chase after shadows, all over the place.

As night falls, the fireflies start their dance,
Their twinkling's a reminder of my lost chance.
I'll blame it on the coconuts' bold spree,
For making a night so chaotic and free.

Vibrant Market in the Heart of Paradise

Lemme tell ya, the market's a scene,
With fruit hats and laughter, oh so obscene.
The mangoes are winking, the papayas tease,
While pineapples giggle in the warm breeze.

I try to haggle, but the prices are high,
The vendors just smile, oh my, oh my!
A lady twirls surreal in her bright muumuu,
As I trip on a basket of bright red tofu.

The smells swirl like a carnival delight,
Fish tacos and spices, what a strange sight.
Between laughter and chaos, I'm lost in the mix,
But oh, get me home before I try to fix!

Roaming Through Fields of Pineapple Gold

In fields of gold with hair like a plant,
I wander and giggle, my grateful chant.
Those prickly fruits wave as I pass on by,
"Don't eat us raw!" they seem to sigh.

I bump into a goat, pondering the view,
He munches on greens like it's all brand new.
We share a silent moment, both in a daze,
The world's just a picnic; it's a silly maze!

With juice on my chin and a smile so wide,
I declare myself ruler of this green ride.
But oh, don't forget, this is how I fail,
When I try to surf aboard a banana sail!

Caribbean Daydream

On a chair, I sit with a drink,
A parrot squawks, don't you think?
The sun is bright, my hat is wide,
In this bliss, I take great pride.

Footprints in the sand, oh dear,
Dancing crabs are drawing near.
With each step, they scuttle fast,
I'll never catch them, not at last.

A coconut falls, I scream and duck,
Right on target, what terrible luck!
A reggae beat shakes the ground,
Why's my drink still not around?

Sunburned nose and tropic breeze,
Can one really have too much cheese?
Amidst the waves, I start to sway,
This daydream won't just fade away.

Crescendo of the Tides

Waves are crashing with a tune,
I try to dance beneath the moon.
My flip-flops fly, they soar so high,
Did they just wave me goodbye?

Seashells scattered, oh what fun,
I've built a castle, but it's all done.
The tide rolls in with quite a dash,
No time to fret, it's gone in a splash!

A fish jumps up, steals my drink,
Am I losing it, what do you think?
With laughter loud and snacks so sweet,
The sand is in my snacks; what a treat!

The beach umbrella's blown away,
In the wind, it starts to sway.
But still, I grin, I've got a ride:
With waves and jokes, I surf the tide.

Tropical Epiphanies

Underneath the palm, I muse,
Why can't I wear all the hues?
Bright colors clash, yet I don't care,
Sunshine and laughter fill the air.

The mango's ripe, a tasty bite,
But rolling off, what a flight!
All the fruits, they play a game,
In this madness, who takes the blame?

As I wade into the sea,
A jellyfish waves back at me.
I wriggle back, the laughter thrives,
These funny critters, oh they jive!

A hammock sways, I try to rest,
But here comes a squirrel, what a pest!
Stealing snacks as I try to nap,
Life's just one big tropical clap!

Scents of the South

The air is thick with sweet desires,
Mango, coconut, and campfire liars.
A barbecue pit, the smoke does rise,
I chase the scent, oh what a prize!

Flip-flops slap against my feet,
A lizard darts; it's quite a feat.
In this heat, I'm feeling brave,
But do they know I've lost my wave?

With a poke, my friend takes a bite,
Of fruit salad that's just out of sight.
What's green and squishy? Try and see!
My tropical dish, it's just for me!

As the sun sets, colors blend,
I laugh and sing, no need to pretend.
With every sip and every bite,
I crown the night, what pure delight!

Sunkissed Bliss

Under palm trees, we dance and sway,
With bright drinks and hats made of hay.
Sunburnt noses, but we don't care,
Laughing at crabs that tug at our hair.

Sandcastles built, but soon they fall,
Time for a nap – oh, we've had a ball!
Seagulls squawking, a cheeky show,
Stealing our chips – oh, the audacity, though!

Rhythm of Rainforest

In the jungle, the monkeys swing,
Stealing snacks, what joy they bring!
Parrots squawk with fabulous flair,
While we trip on roots, free as air.

Raindrops cheer, a slippery dance,
Frogs join in with a ribbiting prance.
Our shoes are soggy, but hearts are light,
Who knew mud could be such a delight?

Starry Coconut Night

Under the stars, we roast our treats,
Laughter rings out as laughter repeats.
Coconuts fall, a thud on the sand,
A coconut drink? Oh, isn't it grand!

With fruity hats, we dance in delight,
Listen to the crickets; they sing through the night.
We may trip over roots, land with a splat,
But oh, the fun of a tropical chat!

Melodies of the Breeze

Breezy whispers in the afternoon glow,
Flapping our shirts as we dance to and fro.
Buzzing bees join our wild, silly song,
While chasing lost flip-flops, we can't go wrong!

Kites in the air with a playful tug,
Caught in a tangle, oh what a shrug!
Sunsets paint clouds a silly hue,
We giggle and snack on sweet mango stew!

The Enchantment of Evening Fireflies

Tiny lights in the soft night,
Dancing around with pure delight.
They blink and they twirl, oh what a sight,
Like nature's stars taking flight.

Catch one quick, but shh, don't scare,
They giggle and wiggle, floating in air.
With tiny giggles, their joy we share,
Be careful, or they'll give you a scare!

A jar in hand for their glow and gleam,
But they plot a tricky little scheme.
They flicker and fade as if in a dream,
Who knew fireflies could be so extreme?

As night closes in, laughter does swell,
With nature's tricks only time will tell.
A bright show of lights, both charming and swell,
Who knew the night could cast such a spell?

Echoes of Waves Against Sandy Shores

Waves crash in rhythm, a foamy dance,
Each one a joke, like nature's romance.
They tickle the toes like a cheeky prance,
Who knew the ocean could take such a chance?

Seagulls squawk as they strut about,
Claiming the beach, there's no doubt.
With a flap and a flap, they shout and scout,
While sunbathers ponder what life's about.

A crab with attitude, pinching away,
Marched right through the sand like it owns the bay.
With its little claws, it's here to stay,
Who said the beach can't be funny in May?

As the sun dips low, an orange parade,
With laughter and waves, the day's serenade.
Under the glow, no worries displayed,
Just echoes of joy and memories made.

Artistry in Nature's Palette

Brushstrokes of green, a vibrant scene,
Colors blend like a dreamer's sheen.
Flowers giggle in hues, so keen,
Nature's party, where life's evergreen.

A bird in a hat, oh, what a sight,
Chirping its tune, a comical flight.
It struts with flair, what a funny plight,
Turns the garden into pure delight.

Beneath shady palms, where giggles grow,
Laughter bounces like seeds in tow.
Nature's canvas, with a whimsical glow,
Each petal a punchline, a floral show.

With a sunset that splashes, bold and bright,
Colors so crazy, they spark pure delight.
In nature's gallery, it's quite a sight,
Who knew the outdoors could tickle just right?

Journey Through Fern-Laden Trails

Winding paths where the ferns play,
They whisper secrets and tease on the way.
With leaves like hands, they give a sway,
Inviting the feet to laugh and stray.

A toad hops by, with a puffed-up chest,
Croaking loud like it's on a quest.
It gives a wink, puts up a jest,
Proclaiming this trail as its very own fest!

Sunlight spills down with a cheerful grin,
Through leafy canopies, the fun begins.
With every step, nature sings within,
A melody of giggles where laughter spins.

At the journey's end, the view's a treat,
With distant mountains, oh such a feat!
Nature chuckles, keeps us on our feet,
A dance of joy, oh what a sweet greet!

Tides of Tranquility

Waves giggle as they lap the shore,
Footprints washed away, who needs more?
Seagulls dive, but miss the fries,
Surfboards wobble, laughter flies.

Sandy toes and sunscreen fights,
Bikini fail, oh what a sight!
Coconut drinks with silly straws,
Cheers to fun and sandy flaws.

Crabs are dancing in the dusk,
Shells parade, it's quite a husk!
A beach ball popped, kids all cry,
But the sun sets, and oh, we sigh.

Mermaids laugh (or so we're told),
In our dreams, we feel so bold.
The tide rolls in, and so must we,
Bringing back this memory.

Floral Melancholy

Petals tumble, it's quite the scene,
Flowers gossip, you know what I mean!
Bees wear shades, they're quite the trend,
But pollen sneezes, they can't pretend.

Sunflowers sway, they chase the sun,
Violets giggle, they're having fun.
A garden party, oh what a sight,
With butterflies dancing, hearts feel light.

Tulips blushing, their colors bright,
But gardeners fuss 'til the fall of night.
Plants with quirks, they'll steal the show,
With secret lives we'll never know.

Roses whisper to the bees,
"Oh dear, watch out for the sneeze!
We bloom so bright, but here's the thing,
A vase without water? Such a sting!

Rhythms of the Rain

Raindrops tap-dance on rooftops high,
Puddles form, oh me, oh my!
Umbrellas twirl, it's quite the game,
Synchronized chaos, who's to blame?

Kids jump in, splashes abound,
Raincoats flapping, laughter's found.
The weather man said "light showers,"
But we're soaked—let's start the hours!

Thunder grumbles; clouds all frown,
While ducks parade in their own gown.
Lightning flickers; what's the rush?
Wading through puddles, oh, such a hush.

In rain-soaked fun, we'll lose our cares,
Fashion faux pas? Who even dares?
A dance of droplets, hearts alive,
In the rhythm of rain, we thrive.

Soundtrack of the Surge

Waves crashing with a joyful boom,
Mixing surf beats, we clear the room.
Seashells clink like little chimes,
Nature's DJ, spinning rhymes.

Palm trees sway, they join the beat,
With every gust, a lively treat.
Surfboards squeak, a silly sound,
As laughter echoes all around.

Fish flip-flop in a frolicking style,
"Join the dance!" they wink with a smile.
Shells applaud from their ocean floor,
Sending rhythms straight to shore.

In this seaside funk, life's never bland,
Just grab your shades, we're making plans.
So let the waves compose our song,
In this funny surge, we all belong.

Tropical Reverie

Palm trees swaying to the beat,
With coconuts falling at my feet.
A parrot squawks a silly tune,
While I dance under the bright moon.

Flip-flops stuck in the sand,
I slip and slide like it's unplanned.
Ice cream melting down my chin,
Who knew a beach could be this thin?

A crab scuttles by with a wink,
While I take another drink.
Sunburned nose, too much sun,
Laughter echoes, oh what fun!

Each sunset a colors clash,
As folks on boards attempt to splash.
Waves crash down, a wet surprise,
And soaked friends laugh till they cry.

Shores of Serenity

Seashells decorating my toes,
Flipping burgers, striking poses.
Seagulls squawking, stealing fries,
I greet them with my best disguise.

Tanning lotion, a slippery mess,
Accident-prone, I must confess.
The hammock swings, but not for long,
I'm airborne now, where did I go wrong?

A game of beach ball, quite the sight,
Three friends diving — it's pure delight!
One lands headfirst, oh what a splash,
While the others laugh in a muddash!

The sun goes down, we're all aglow,
In flip-flops searching for the show.
A fire pit with marshmallows near,
Who knew staying here would bring such cheer?

Tropical Odyssey

Aqua waters, a vivid dream,
Sailing further, or so it seems.
With a pirate parrot on my hat,
I sway and wiggle, just like that!

Fishing lines full of socks,
Unfished bait, oh what a paradox!
The boat flips, a comical thrill,
Me flailing about, I can't keep still.

Sunburned and ruffled, what a sight,
Diving for treasure feels just right!
The only gold? A rusty old can,
It's as worthless as any old plan!

Yet here I am, searching anew,
For seaweed snacks – oh, who knew?
It's a feast fit for the mermaid crew,
Sailing away, just me and my stew.

Sun-drenched Memories

A beach ball bounces to the tide,
Chasing thoughts we can't abide.
Picnic snacks, they're now awry,
Seagulls plotting, oh my, oh my!

A golden tan, a little too bold,
Friends keep laughing, what a hold!
Building castles, all in jest,
Watch the waves claim our best test.

Sandy sandwiches, what a treat,
A crumbly mess, can't be beat.
I slip on sunscreen, whoops, my eye!
Now I'm swimming, oh my, oh my!

With each sunset, laughter echoes loud,
As the tide adds to our joyous crowd.
Sun-drenched days turn into tales,
Of silly grins and happy trails.

Petals and Spice in the Ocean Air

Roses dance in winds so fair,
Giggling flowers, without a care.
Coconut trees sway side to side,
Waves tickle toes, we all glide.

Laughter jumps like dolphins bright,
Underneath the sun's warm light.
Mangoes smile from the trees,
While parrots crack jokes with ease.

Seashells whisper stories old,
As the sun paints skies with gold.
Ukuleles strum a tune,
Even the crabs are in a swoon.

Bananas slip with playful grace,
Drawing smiles on every face.
In this land of sun and cheer,
Every moment's filled with beer!

The Language of Laughter Among Friends

Friends gather 'neath the palm trees,
Jokes float on the gentle breeze.
Sipping drinks with tiny straws,
Pointing out each funny flaw.

A parrot squawks a silly rhyme,
While we all lose track of time.
Sandcastles rise, then tumble down,
Water splashes, no one frowns.

Sunsets bring a canvas bright,
As laughter dances in the light.
With every wave, the giggles grow,
And even crabs join in the show.

We toast to joy, we raise our glass,
As goofy moments come to pass.
In this paradise, we embark,
Live life fully, just like a lark!

Tropical Whispers

Whispers drift on the salty air,
Mangoes flirt without a care.
Bananas giggle, swing and sway,
While the sun shines bright all day.

Coconuts crack a joke so sweet,
Under the shade, friends all meet.
The ocean hums a silly song,
As we dance and all sing along.

Breezes carry stories told,
Of silly days and nights so bold.
Laughter echoes 'midst the trees,
Time pauses with such easy tease.

Even the fish swim with glee,
In this land where we're all free.
With every wave, our spirits lift,
This life here is the greatest gift!

Sunlit Shores

Sunlit shores call to our feet,
With each step, our joy's complete.
The sand tickles, a gentle tease,
As we roll and bask in ease.

Shells and seaweed play their part,
Crafting laughter, pure and smart.
Caught in a wave, what a surprise,
Our hilarity reaches the skies!

Dancing crabs with shifty moves,
They compete with our silly grooves.
Drinks topple over, splashes fly,
While seagulls squawk and pass us by.

As day fades, the stars awake,
Making plans for pranks we'll make.
In this joyous, sunlit place,
Life's a dance, a laughter race!

Jungle Heartbeat

In the jungle, vines do dance,
Monkeys plotting their next prance.
A toucan yells, "Hey, look at me!"
While I trip on roots, so carefree.

Parrots squawk, their jokes are loud,
Cocohut hats, I'm feeling proud.
Lemurs leap with such a flair,
As my flip-flop flies through the air!

Underneath the leafy drape,
I find myself in quite a scrape.
The gators laugh, I swear they grin,
Guess it's my turn for a splashy spin!

So here's to laughter, wild and free,
In every slip, there's joy, you see.
In the jungle, life's a hoot,
Especially when you're chasing fruit!

Solitude in Sunshine

On a beach where seagulls squawk,
I sunbathe like a lazy rock.
Sunblock slathered, I lay wide,
While crabs come up for a fun ride!

I sip my drink and spill it too,
As a wave sneaks up, oh what a view!
My towel's gone, flown off in glee,
Chased by a dog, now it's chasing me!

Sandcastles built with shaky hands,
Soon crumble down like optimistic plans.
A kid yells, "Dude, get a grip!"
Falling sideways, I take a dip!

But in the sun, all worries fade,
As laughter echoes in this parade.
So here's to fun, with a splash and cheer,
Life's better when you let go of fear!

Fragrant Petals

In a garden where flowers bloom,
I stop and stare, lost in their plume.
Bees buzzing like they own the day,
While I'm tripping through, in dismay.

A rose cheekily steals my hat,
As daisies giggle, "What's up with that?"
Lavender waves with a fragrant shout,
Didn't see the thorn, now I must pout!

Butterflies flicker, spread their flair,
While I dance like I don't have a care.
But every step makes petals flee,
And the tulips chant, "Oh don't be me!"

Still, I twirl, no room for frowns,
Amongst the colors, I wear my crowns.
So here's to blooms and silly quests,
Life's a garden; take your rest!

Echoes of the Surf

Waves crash in a rhythmic beat,
As I try to catch my feet.
Surfboards topple, giggles fly,
While jellyfish wave their gooey, hi!

Sandy sandwiches stuck in hair,
And salty water's all I wear.
A crab scuttles, tries to race,
While I lose my shoes without a trace!

Seagulls dive, plotting my snack,
While I struggle to stay on track.
Jumping waves, oh what a sight,
Until I crash, then take flight!

Yet in this chaos, laughter reigns,
As each splash brings silly gains.
In echoes loud, the surf does sing,
Of joy, mishaps, and everything!

The Sweet Aroma of Sea and Spice

The fish dance in their spicy coat,
As I try to catch one on a boat.
The sea salt tickles my nose,
Why does the chef add so much prose?

Coconut hats and pineapples sway,
I wear my food, come what may!
A crab scuttles by in a hurry,
I trip and laugh, oh what a flurry!

Coconut Cradle of the Ocean's Song

In a hammock made of palm leaves wide,
Bouncing like a boat on a joyride.
The coconut falls with a thud,
Hey! That's not a snack, that's my bud!

I sip from a shell, feeling quite grand,
While jellyfish jiggle, oh how they stand!
The sun spills gold on my funny bone,
With beach vibes that feel like home, unknown.

Where the Coral Meets the Sky

Fish wear sunglasses and strut their stuff,
The coral reef says, "What's up, tough?"
A dolphin leaps, off on a quest,
While I ponder which snack is the best.

Clouds above look like cotton candy,
And seagulls squawk sounding quite dandy.
A starfish waves, it's not shy,
He's teaching me to wave, oh my!

Tides of Laughter and Lush Green

Bamboo shoots peek from the jungle's edge,
While monkeys swing, giving me a pledge.
"I'll share my banana, just take a seat!"
I think to myself, "What a tasty treat!"

The waves tickle toes, laughter fills the air,
It seems even crabs know how to share.
I trip on a shell, oh silly me,
The ocean's alive with such glee!

Chasing Horizons

In flip-flops we run, oh what a sight,
Chasing waves like children, pure delight.
Seagulls squawk loudly, they laugh at our moves,
While sunscreen drips down in the heat that soothes.

We built our castles near the shoreline,
But with every big wave, we lose our design.
Sand stuck to noses, we giggle and squeal,
Who needs fine art when this is our deal?

The sun sets like pizza, all melted and round,
Colors like candy spread out on the ground.
With each silly dance, our joys overflow,
Life's just a beach party, don't you know?

So come join the madness, bring laughter and cheer,
With every good joke, let's banish the fear.
We'll chase down horizons, our fun never ends,
In this sandy kingdom where everyone's friends.

Warming Sunbeams

Oh, the warming sunbeams, they tickle my nose,
Golden rays giggle, and everyone knows.
With drinks in our hands, we toast to the day,
As ice cubes do dances and slowly sway.

The beach chairs recline, a perfect parade,
While umbrellas act like soldiers in jade.
I try to stand up but my legs turn to jelly,
A plop in the sand, oh, my poor little belly!

We play ball with coconuts, oh what a game,
But dodging the splash makes us all look insane.
Laughter erupts as someone gets splashed,
Who knew that the ocean could be so brash?

So, grab all your pals, let's soak in this cheer,
In sunbeams that warm while we drink our cold beer.
With goofy grins shared, let's dance to the beat,
In this tropical realm, life feels like a treat.

Soothing Sprays

Sprays of the ocean serenade the shore,
With each bubbly giggle, we're craving for more.
We leap like the dolphins, we glide like the sun,
In this splashy play, we all feel like one.

Each wave brings a tickle, a slap on our backs,
We dodge and we weave, feeling intrepid attacks.
The breeze plays a trick, it snatches my hat,
Caught on a wave, oh! Have you seen that?

The crabs march like soldiers across on the sand,
They scuttle so fast, I can barely withstand.
But one quick grab showed their sneaky little plan,
Now I'm cradling crabs, oh, the world of the tan!

Soothing sprays call out, let's jump in the fun,
Where laughter is floating like rays from the sun.
In this wavy kingdom, we live out a tale,
With giggles and splashes, we'll never grow stale.

Luminary of the Limelight

Beneath the bright sky, we gather for play,
With our hats on our heads, what a scene on display.
The limelight is shining, but it's not just the sun,
It's us with our antics, bringing joy by the ton!

With surfboards we ride, our balance quite shaky,
The wipeouts are epic, oh they're such a fakey!
I tried to impress but just fell on my face,
An audience gathered, oh what a disgrace!

The parrots above shout their praises and jeers,
As we pretend luscious fruit turns into our beers.
We dance like the fish, all slippery and sly,
In this limelight of laughter, we all learn to fly.

So, grab all your pals, let's put on a show,
With giggles and spritzes, we steal the whole glow.
In this world of bright colors, life isn't so tight,
We're luminaries now, shining with all our might!

Embrace of the Sundrenched Horizon

The sun is hot, the beach is loud,
Seagulls squawk, they form a crowd.
Flip-flops flop, as I descend,
To find the towel—and likely bend.

My drink's a mix of fruit and cheer,
It tastes like joy but looks like beer!
I sip too fast, it goes too low,
And now my sunhat tends to flow!

The sand's a trap for my two feet,
Each grain a thief, they make retreat.
I try to walk, it's quite a sight,
Who knew the beach could cause a fight?

So here I stand, a sunburned clown,
With sunscreen blobs, I wear a crown.
Embracing warmth in wild delight,
While jellyfish float, well, out of sight!

Colorful Kites Soaring with the Wind

Up in the sky, the colors clash,
Kites dance around—oh, what a splash!
One drops its tail, it dives for fun,
And loops with flair, my hat is gone!

They waltz and swirl, a vibrant sight,
While I just stand, my grip is tight.
A paper dragon steals my lunch,
In this wild game, I've lost my punch!

The breeze is strong, it pulls and tugs,
Kite strings tangled like loveable bugs.
I laugh and shout, a joyful fight,
As windcrash echoes through the light!

Oh playful skies, with your mad ballet,
You turn a picnic to a fray.
Kite-flyers cheer, while I just grin,
Who knew this chaos could begin?

Lush Layers Beneath the Sunshine

In the garden deep, I find a bite,
A sandwich lost, it shone too bright.
With critters nibbled, it now decays,
Nature's lunch gone bold in ways!

The veggies wave their leafy arms,
Like hippies grooving with subtle charms.
Tomatoes blush, salsa on edge,
As herbs get fancy in their hedge!

Flowers giggle, petals in prime,
They mock the bees, oh, what a crime!
A garden dance, the sun's their cue,
While I just watch and try to chew.

In this vibrant realm, things often sway,
Where weeds wear crowns and skies are gray.
I'll take a break, then join the song,
As I trip on roots—life's never wrong!

Rippled Reflections of a Lazy Lagoon

The lagoon's calm, with fish that prance,
   While I attempt my best to dance.
  Each step I take, the ripples spread,
   And splash a frog right on the head!

Drifting dreams float on the breeze,
   I try to paddle—oh, the tease!
  The boat's a tub, a floating mess,
  With wobbly moves, I lose my dress!

The sun is setting, colors blur,
   Paddle flops, I'm in a stir.
  Reflections laugh, my hair's a 'do,
That says, "I'm lost, how 'bout you?"

As laughter echoes in this space,
I greet the fish, they know my face.
  In lazy waters, life's a game,
Where nothing works, but still—no shame!

Kaleidoscope of Flora

In a garden of colors, oh what a sight,
A parrot named Pete took a flower to flight.
He wore a big hat, it was quite the show,
While the petals protested, they just couldn't glow.

The daisies were dreaming, their heads in a spin,
As Pete tied them up, now they're ready to win.
Butterflies giggled, they danced on the breeze,
Chasing their tails, just as they pleased.

The roses were blushing, their charm on display,
While daisies asked, "Why can't we play?"
"Oh dear," said Pete, "Let the fun now commence,
Or we'll end this madness—it just don't make sense!"

Let's sip on some nectar, let's start a parade,
With a gopher named Gary—who's really afraid.
He danced with the leaves but tripped on a vine,
Now he juggles the tulips—oh, what a fine line!

Paradise Found

In a beach hut of dreams, with a view oh so wide,
A crab named Carl claimed the whole sandy tide.
He brought out his pals—yes, the shells in a row,
    To dance like a conga and put on a show.

With seagulls a-squawking, they formed a parade,
While Carl waved his claws—"Hey, pass the lemonade!"
The starfish just chuckled, they joined in the sway,
    As the turtles got lost trying to find their way.

The sun-loungers cheered, as the coconut fell,
    Landing straight on Carl—now he's in a shell!
He laughed and he splashed, in the ocean's embrace,
    With the fish just a-peeking, it's a party, not a race.

So join in the fun, let the good vibes abound,
With Carl and his buddies in this paradise found.
In the warmth of the sun, where the laughter is free,
    Come dance on the beach, who cares about sea!

Winds of Change

Up in the palm trees, the monkeys conspire,
To swing on the breeze, with a goal to go higher.
They flipped and they flopped, such a comical sight,
One slipped on a coconut and gave quite a fright.

In the jungle's embrace, with the winds in their fur,
They plotted a scheme with a splash and a purr.
"We'll ride on the zephyrs, and dance in the hues,
Just watch for the parrots—they've got the good news."

They twirled through the ferns, on a merry-go-round,
Spinning leaves with their tales, making mischief abound.

The sunbeams did giggle, as the breeze made them sway,
With a whirl and a twirl—oh, what a day!

As clouds turned to pillows, a party took flight,
Creating a ruckus, what a sheer delight!
Amidst all the chaos, a lesson remained,
That fun in the jungle means laughter unchained!

Kaleidoscopic Sunsets

As daylight drifts down, the colors collide,
A flamingo named Fiona joins the wild slide.
She flaps her pink wings, all the hues in a dance,
Belly flopping, she giggles, as she takes a chance.

The horizon erupts, with oranges and blues,
While a parrot named Pete sings the sunset blues.
With the waves gently crashing, they cheerfully cheer,
"Here comes the night, let's give it a cheer!"

The clouds twirl and twist, like a whimsical show,
With starfish down below waving "Hey, don't be slow!"
A crab joins the chorus, with a pinch of delight,
As the colors explode and the world feels just right.

So gather your friends for this glorious spree,
Under kaleidoscopic skies, so silly and free.
We'll laugh with the sunset, as evening comes near,
Join us in joy as we toast with good cheer!

Driftwood Dreams

Once a log wrote a letter, to a fish in despair,
It wished for a buddy, to swim without care.
The fish started laughing, said, "You're a dry mess!"
"But you float like a king, no need to impress!"

Manta rays held a party, with snacks from the sea,
But seagulls crashed in, just to steal all the glee.
They grabbed all the chips, and flew off in a caper,
Leaving the rays with some blubbering paper.

Coconuts in a hammock, they tied with a line,
Hoping they'd catch a few drinks, maybe wine.
Instead, they got milk, with a splash and a grin,
And toasted to parties in the sun and the wind.

So if you're ever drifting, on a log or a dream,
Remember the fish and the rays that they scheme.
Life's a funny ocean, with giggles and sways,
Where laughter finds company, in the sun's warm rays.

Lagoon of Luminescence

In a hidden lagoon, where the jellyfish dance,
The crabs held a contest, for the best sea prance.
Last year's champ flailed, with a move called the flop,
But mermaids just laughed, and said, "Look at that drop!"

The turtles wore shades, as they lounged on a rock,
"Life's too short," one said, "for a sea turtle clock!"
They discussed fancy dishes, like seaweed à la mode,
While the fish swam in circles, fashionable road.

A pelican strolled by, with a hat far too big,
Claiming it's perfect for catching a gig.
The squids rolled their eyes; he had feathers, not flair,
Yet he strutted so proud, like he hadn't a care.

Underneath the moon's glow, everything sparkled,
Like laughter in the night, where water is marled.
So next time you wander, on shores or in dreams,
Remember the fun, and the laughter that beams.

Wildflower Whimsy

In a field of wildflowers, a bee lost its way,
It chatted with daisies, who just wanted to play.
"You smell like sweet candy!" the petals all chimed,
While the bee buzzed about, like it's perfectly timed.

A butterfly flapped, wearing polka dot shoes,
It claimed it was fashion, and nothing to lose.
The flowers just chuckled, said, "Darling, so chic!
But don't wear them in rain; it's the last thing you seek!"

The frogs threw a contest, for the best belly flop,
But the flowers kept giggling, "Will someone please stop?"
While crickets synchronized, in their evening ballet,
The field became laughter, dancing night away.

So if you find petals, where laughter blooms free,
Join the wildflower waltz, sing in harmony.
For nature's a funny place, with joy as its theme,
Where whimsy and silliness dance just like a dream.

Secrets of the Shore

The sea's got its secrets, tucked under the foam,
Like a crab that can't walk, but insists it's at home.
With a pinch and a scuttle, it's king of the rocks,
While seagulls are plotting, in their comical flocks.

A fish wore a suit, with a bowtie so neat,
While the octopus grinned, offering snacks to eat.
"Just lumber by slowly," the sea turtle said,
"Dress fancy for dinner, not a long swim ahead!"

A clam held a meeting, declaring a doubt,
"How do we avoid getting taken out?"
They all shared a giggle, and planned for the day,
"To hide with a seaweed, come what may!"

So if you wander shores, and hear whispers of glee,
Know the creatures are laughing, quite wild and carefree.
Their secrets are treasures, adorned with bright cheer,
Where fun floats like bubbles, and life's always near.

Serenade of the Tropical Breeze

The palm trees sway, a comical dance,
As coconuts tumble, given a chance.
A pineapple croons a silly old tune,
While monkeys swing by, howling at the moon.

Breezes tickle the noses on the beach,
While sunburned tourists complain and screech.
A crab in a sombrero scuttles around,
Crafting a fiesta from shells that he found.

Seagulls squawk jokes in their feathery glee,
Stealing chips from a kid on a spree.
Laughter erupts, like waves on the shore,
In this tropical land, who could ask for more?

So bring on the laughter, the joy, and the fun,
Where the breeze whispers tales beneath the sun.
A verse of oddities fills the salty air,
In this goofy paradise, let troubles beware!

Nectar of the Wild Hibiscus

Once there was flower with a curious face,
Who thought it could use a bit more grace.
It wore a hat made of buzzing bees,
And offered them nectar with playful pleas.

The bees got tipsy, forgot their way home,
And decided to party, no need to roam.
They danced on petals, a wild, silly sight,
Painting the garden in colors so bright.

Butterflies giggled, joining the fun,
As they fluttered in circles, basking in sun.
The hibiscus blushed, feeling quite grand,
As it ruled over its vibrant land.

With laughter in petals, and buzz in the air,
A nectar that tickles without a care.
This flower's a joker, one of its kinds,
In a garden of humor, where laughter unwinds!

Colorful Feathers in the Midday Sun

Parrots in shades of a painter's palette,
Chatter away like they own the gallet.
With jokes about seeds and a mock of a squawk,
They strut their stuff on the high ocean rock.

A toucan misplaced his beak of bright hue,
Claimed it was stolen by a parakeet crew.
The flock laughed so hard, they fell off the tree,
Turning the scene into pure slapstick spree.

In a wig of grasses, a lizard had flair,
Pretending to be a flamboyant heir.
With a wiggle and jiggle, he stole the show,
While nearby, a turtle said, "Oh no, no!"

So here's to the birds with their carefree chimes,
In the sun-soaked air, they spin funny rhymes.
With feathers and giggles, they paint the scene,
In this lighthearted world, where laughter's the queen!

Dance of Shadows on Golden Sand

At dusk the shadows begin to prance,
On grains of gold, they twist and dance.
A crab in a tutu takes center stage,
While a starfish jokes, "I'm quite the sage!"

The sun dips low, beach balls go crazy,
A kid with ice cream is feeling quite hazy.
Seagulls throw shade, making quite the fuss,
Saying, "We know who's really in charge of us!"

A towel-flapping breeze joins the delight,
As the night steals the show, with glittering light.
While jellyfish glow, holding a rave,
It's a shadowy party, so come on and wave!

With laughter echoing through this wild night,
Where lights twinkle like stars, oh what a sight!
In this dance of shadows, let spirits soar,
For in the tropical air, who could ask for more?

Ecstasy of the Elements

The sun kissed my forehead, so bright and bold,
A crab tried to steal my sandwich, I'm told.
The waves whispered secrets, oh what a chat,
While palm trees danced, wearing coconut hats.

The breeze brought laughter, it tickled my toes,
The seagulls joined in with their funny crows.
Sandy toes wiggled, freeing some grime,
Beach towels flapped like they were in mime.

The clouds joined the party, they brought some rain,
I slipped on a flip-flop, oh what a pain!
But laughter erupted; it bounced off the tide,
In this silly paradise, what joy I abide!

So let's raise a toast to the elements here,
With a splash of the ocean, and a can of beer.
Life's quirks are the essence, of this warm sunny place,
Where the absurdity of nature fills every space.

Harbor of Hope

In a harbor of wishes, where boats float and sway,
I asked a fat dolphin, could he dance ballet?
He laughed as he splashed, with a flip and a twist,
While my dreams set sail, like the sun in the mist.

The fisherman chuckled, his bait was a shoe,
He claimed it attracted the fish that flew.
As seabirds paraded in splendid array,
The harbor was jolly, come join the play!

With shells as my treasure, I stacked them so high,
A crab became king, with a royal sigh.
The tide pulled my dreams, like a mischievous tide,
In this place full of giggles, all worries subside.

So let's toast to the harbor, where hope's in the breeze,
With laughter and quirks that aim to please.
Where every odd moment is gold in disguise,
And the sea keeps your secrets, like fun little lies.

Skimming the Surface

I skipped on the water, well, kind of, I tried,
But plopped like a penguin, with belly so wide.
The fish rolled their eyes, as they swam by with glee,
While a turtle just chuckled, saying, "Look at me!"

The sun played a prank, it blazed from afar,
While I searched my pockets for sunscreen, my star.
But found only jellybeans and an old flip-flop,
As my tan turned to crimson, I wanted to stop.

The waves threw a party, with bubbles and foam,
I vowed I'll be careful, but then I lost my comb.
A sea snake approached, with a wink and a grin,
"Are you here for the dance? Come join in the din!"

So here's to the water, where laughter runs free,
In the splashes of joy, I find parts of me.
With a giggle and chuckle, I'm skimming away,
In this hullabaloo under the sun's bright ray.

Isles of Inspiration

In the isles of my daydreams, where bananas wear shades,

And pineapples dance like they're ready for parades.
Each hut sings its tune, with a rickety beat,
As lizards strut by, all decked out, on fleet.

I spotted a parrot dressed up like a queen,
With jewels made of breadcrumbs, she ruled pristine.
Her subjects were crabs in a conga line,
Grooving to rhythms, oh what a fine time!

The air's thick with laughter, it floats on the breeze,
A surfboard took flight, and it landed with ease.
My tropical fantasies twist like a vine,
In this land full of chuckles, where all things align.

So here's to the islands, where humor's the key,
Every nook and cranny where joy likes to flee.
With coconuts laughing and sunshine so bright,
Let's dance with the waves 'til the fall of the night.

Symphony of Tides

The waves dance with a silly swagger,
Shells giggle as they bounce and stagger.
Crabs in bow ties tap their claws,
While starfish applaud with their eight small paws.

Seagulls squawk a tuneful song,
As jellyfish party all night long.
An octopus leads with a jazzy flair,
While fish on the floor just shake their hair.

Palm trees sway to the beachy beat,
Where sunburnt tourists shuffle their feet.
A dolphin's leap—a comical sight,
Splashing water, what a delight!

But watch your sandwich, don't let it fly,
The seagulls are sneaky and oh-so spry.
With each wave crashing, they all sing loud,
Nature's orchestra, a vibrant crowd!

Vibrant Dusk

As sun dips low, the sky turns pink,
The parrot's jokes make us all rethink.
Laughter echoes through the coconut trees,
While monkeys throw peanuts with expert ease.

A toucan struts, with a colorful grin,
Saying, 'What about trivia? Who'll take me in?'
The crickets chirp their evening tune,
While fireflies blink, under the silver moon.

Here comes a lizard in a tiny hat,
Claiming he's cool, and he can do this and that.
But as he trips on a thirsty vine,
We all know he's just a lizard in line!

The stars above wink their bright eyes,
As palm fronds wave and laughter flies.
In this paradise, it's hard not to cheer,
To the vibrant dusk that brings us near.

Celestial Lagoon

In a lagoon where the colors collide,
A grouper named Gary takes us for a ride.
With shades on his eyes, he's quite the sight,
Leading the swim party into the night.

The water's a mirror, reflecting the fun,
As frogs wear tuxedos and dance one by one.
Crickets in tutus, join in the groove,
While a turtle keeps time with a slick, slow move.

Waves splash gently, holding laughter tight,
And mermaids complain; it's just too bright!
A clumsy seal joins to show off his flips,
He belly flops while the dolphin just tips.

Stars twinkle brightly overhead,
As fish finish their joke about balls of bread.
In this lagoon, with a giggle and cheer,
We soak up the joy, stay close to the dear.

Warmth of Sand

Oh, the sand is warm, like a cozy bed,
Where crabs wear flip-flops as they go ahead.
The sun loungers gossip, what a wild scene,
As flamingos strut, dressed in vibrant sheen.

A beachball rolls, just escaping a kid,
While parents sip drinks and try to outbid.
"Whatcha got?" says a crab with a wink,
While seagulls plot mischief with a smirk and a stink.

Bucket castles rise, but watch out for waves,
The sea's tricky, with all of its braves.
But who can resist the sun's golden embrace,
Or the dance of a pelican in a race?

Under blue skies, with laughter so grand,
We cherish the moments in this sandy land.
As the day ends with a colorful blend,
We wave to the tide, our seasonal friend!

Sand Between Toes

The beach is calling, can't you see?
My flip-flops left, now here's debris!
Each grain of sand's a tiny friend,
They cling to me, will they ever end?

I tiptoe back to the sandcastle throne,
My royal seat made of driftwood and foam.
But oh! A wave comes with a sneaky splash,
Now my throne's a soggy, salty mash!

Seagulls giggle, they steal my snack,
Chasing them off, I've got no knack!
They soar above with beaks so bold,
While I'm windswept and slightly cold.

A hermit crab waves as it scuttles away,
"Don't mind me," it seems to say!
I wave back, it's a silly affair,
Right here, the laughter floats in the air!

Cherished Currents

Tidal waves giggle, rolling in light,
Splashing my toes, what a goofy sight!
The surfboards dance, they bounce and dip,
While I'm over here, taking a slip!

Palm trees sway to the calypso beat,
Shaking their leaves with rhythm so sweet.
I try to join in, swinging my hips,
But alas! I fall and do a few flips!

The sun beams down, playing a game,
It hides behind clouds, then shouts my name!
"Hey there, friend! Are you having fun?"
I chuckle, "Sure, but I'm on the run!"

Coconuts giggle, rolling with glee,
"Come close!" they shout, "Just you wait and see!"
A drink that's sweet, with a silly twist,
In this merry land, I can't resist!

Emerald Canopy

Beneath the leaves, the monkeys swing,
Chasing dreams as they start to sing.
Their antics wild, a joyful spree,
Who knew trees held such a party spree?

A toucan struts with colors bright,
As I sip coconut, what a sight!
The parrot squawks a tune askew,
Wonder if he knows what's proper to do?

Lizards lounge, sunbathing well,
With tiny sunglasses, it's quite a sell.
The whole forest's a comedy show,
Watch your snacks, they might steal your dough!

Even the sloths have a lazy grin,
Too slow to race, they never win.
Yet they twirl with style in their own lane,
Who knew chill could be this insane?

Ocean's Embrace

The waves roll in like a playful pup,
Twisting surfboards like a hiccup.
Seagulls laugh, dive for a snack,
But watch your chips or they'll steal your pack!

A crab in shorts, what a sight to behold,
Dancing on the shore, all brave and bold.
His little moves, quite the routine,
Together, they're a comedic scene!

Sandy toes and sunburned noses,
Collecting shells, where ocean poses.
Oh no! My hat is caught in a breeze,
Looks like seagulls have a taste for cheese!

As sunset paints with strokes of gold,
Beachside stories from young and old.
Laughter rings out, a joyful choir,
With every wave, a fun-filled desire!

Lush Dreams

In fields of green, I bounce around,
Tripping on roots that are easily found.
Butterflies giggle, flutter by,
While I'm still trying not to cry!

A parakeet tells a joke or two,
The punchline's lost, but we're laughing, too.
Grasshoppers join, they hop and cheer,
A garden party filled with glee, my dear!

Rain starts to dance with playful drops,
Jumping puddles as the laughter pops.
"Slip and slide," the frogs all shout,
Until I fall flat, that's what it's about!

The sun resumes, a radiant glow,
Nature's laughter continues to flow.
In this green paradise, I adore,
Every day brings a giggle galore!

Island Serenade

On sandy shores, ukuleles play,
Turtles bobbing in a gentle sway.
With sing-alongs from shells so grand,
Who knew sea creatures were in a band?

A hula dancer spins all around,
Her skirt is grass, what a sight unbound!
The breeze joins in, sways with delight,
She tripped on her toes, oh what a fright!

Beneath the palms, the coconuts fall,
Don't stand too close, you might take a call!
The main attraction, I must confess,
Is when fruit hits heads, oh the mess!

As the moon rises in the evening air,
Fireflies twinkle without a care.
A cosmic show on this island stage,
Laughter roams free, in this fun-filled page!

Harmonies of Home

In the hut where the roosters sleep,
A coconut's dream is far from deep.
Banana peels slip, a dance on the floor,
Laughter erupts, as we slide out the door.

Palm trees sway, doing the cha-cha,
Crabs join in, what a wild extra.
The beach ball bounces, our choreographed fate,
Who knew the tide could be so late?

Sipping on juice, face painted like art,
Someone's hat flies, a comical start.
We wave goodbye to the sunscreen spray,
All in good fun, in our own crazy way.

The sun sets low, a stage for our show,
With flip-flop taps, we take a curious bow.
In this crazy place, where the laughter is bold,
We find silly treasures, more precious than gold.

Sheltered Shores

Waves whisper secrets to a beach so bright,
Seashells applaud with a shimmer of light.
Seagulls squawk loudly, a comedic Choir,
While a barbecue's smoke dances higher and higher.

Coolers are packed with the oddest of snacks,
Fishy surprises leap out of their packs.
A picnic unfolds with sandwiches spry,
But the ants march in as if they'll fly.

The sun takes a dive, perfect for frogs,
Slippery slides made of inflatable logs.
Splashing and laughing, topsy-turvy glee,
Chasing seagulls is quite the spree!

Stars twinkle down on our wonky parade,
And sand in our toes is the price we've paid.
With every mishap, we're glued at the seams,
Creating a canvas of wobbly dreams.

Hidden Cove Haven

Tucked where the land and the sea blend like paint,
Oh, what a joy where the treasures ain't faint!
Boulders that giggle when waves go a'woo,
And crabs have their gossip, as neighbors do too.

A hammock sways softly, a nap's on the list,
But mosquitoes have other plans in their mist.
Gnarly old palm trees wave back with a wink,
As we try to balance on our drink-toting sink.

Under the rocks, an octopus peeks,
With eight fuzzy arms, isn't that what one seeks?
We chuckle with dolphins that leap by our side,
In this whimsical world, we stumble and glide.

The setting sun packs a colorful punch,
As laughter spills over the evening's sweet brunch.
In this cove where the giggles ignite,
Finding joy all around, everything feels right.

The Calm Before the Storm

Butterflies flutter, sky looks a tad green,
Chickens are clucking like they've lost their routine.
The breeze whispers secrets, quite playful, you see,
While squirrels prepare their own mystery spree.

Sunblock's forgotten; the clouds have conspired,
Each fish in the sea seems a bit more wired.
The wind teases hair, like a rebellious foe,
As surfboards shuffle, ready to go.

Straws blown by gusts into spaces absurd,
Someone's hat flys off—oh, how it has stirred!
The coconut drinks tip and begin their own dance,
This pre-storm excitement makes us all glance.

When thunder rolls in and laughter ignites,
We gather together for stormy delights.
And as raindrops start, in a giddy old rush,
We twirl in the puddles, a rambunctious hush.

www.ingramcontent.com/pod-product-compliance
Lightning Source LLC
Chambersburg PA
CBHW072214070526
44585CB00015B/1338